The Three Bears

by Sharon Fear
illustrated by Buket

Scott Foresman

Editorial Offices: Glenview, Illinois • New York, New York
Sales Offices: Reading, Massachusetts • Duluth, Georgia
Glenview, Illinois • Carrollton, Texas • Menlo Park, California

There were three bears.
They lived in a little house.

They had three bowls . . .

and three chairs...

and three beds.

But one day. . .

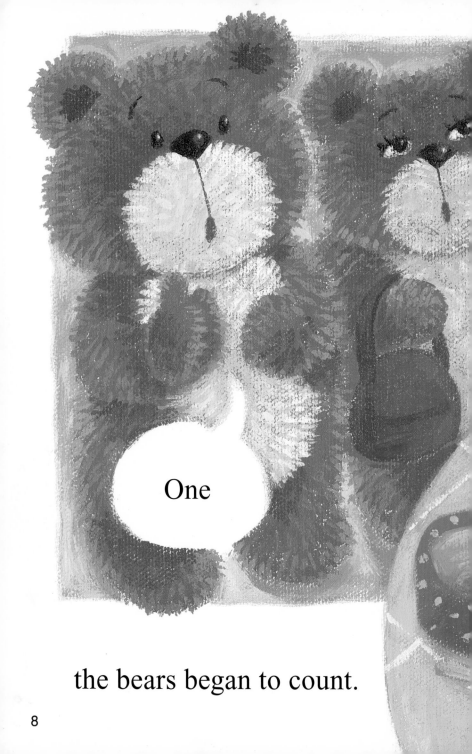

One

the bears began to count.

There were four bowls!

There were four chairs!

There were four beds!

Oops!

There were three bears.

They lived in a little house.

But not in this little house!